A lively Boudicca riding in her chariot on this weathervane at Quidenham, Norfolk, matches a similar depiction on the village sign.

WEATHERVANES

Patricia and Philip Mockridge

Shire Publications Ltd

CONTENTS

Published in 1997 by Shire Publications Ltd, Cromwell House, Church Street, Princes Risborough, Buckinghamshire HP27 9AA, UK. Copyright © 1993 by Patricia Mockridge. First published 1993, reprinted 1997. Shire Album 291. ISBN 0 7478 0191 6.

Printed in Great Britain by CIT Printing Services, Press Buildings, Merlins Bridge, Haverfordwest, Pembrokeshire SA61 1XF.

British Library Cataloguing in Publication Data: Mockridge, Patricia. Weathervanes. — (Shire Albums; No. 291). I. Title. II. Mockridge, Philip. III. Series. 739. ISBN 0-7478-0191-6.

ACKNOWLEDGEMENTS
The authors acknowledge help from museum and library staff, the public relations officers of businesses and local government, church representatives, custodians and private owners. They particularly thank the makers of weathervanes – artist and craftsman blacksmiths, foundries and amateurs. All have been endlessly patient and instructive. The authors are particularly grateful to all the people who allowed access to normally inaccessible vantage points within private boundaries in order to take photographs.

Cover: *Alice, the White Rabbit and the Mad Hatter, beneath a finial of a benign Cheshire Cat, are a charming reminder of Lewis Carroll at Daresbury, Cheshire, his birthplace.*

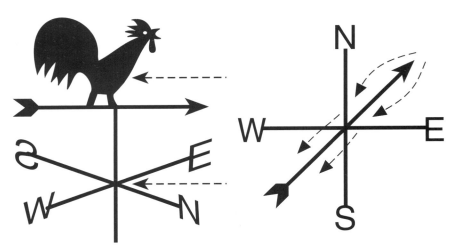

Diagrams showing how the most familiar type of weathervane responds to wind direction: (left) side view; (right) plan. In this case there is a north-east wind (the wind is blowing from the north-east). The air current catches the tail of the weathervane, sending it back, while the arrow-head, which has a smaller surface area, comes round and points into the wind. Hence the weathervane indicates a north-east wind.

PAST AND PRESENT

The word 'weathervane', though universally understood, is a misnomer: the objects are more accurately called wind vanes, since they respond solely to wind direction. The weathervanes with which we are most familiar point upwind, that is, towards the wind that is blowing. Confusingly, however, some do exactly the opposite and point downwind, away from it.

This apparent contradiction arises partly, as will become evident, from the historical influences that have shaped weathervanes. However, recognising whether any particular example points upwind or downwind is in practice very easy: the larger surface area will be downwind. The simplest weathervane shape looks and works exactly like a metal flag (for example, Chichester, West Sussex); we have no difficulty accepting that it blows downwind. But, especially since the eighteenth century, most such flag vanes have been balanced by streamlined arrow pointers pointing upwind. Our eyes are so attuned to arrows that they instinctively 'read' these pointers and relegate the 'flag' information (Tower of London).

Whatever creature, object or scene replaces the flag, the same principle operates: the smaller end points upwind, the larger is a tail, indicating downwind. Very few are seriously confusing.

This wind-swivelled *motif* is the first and indeed the only indispensable one of the six main elements that any weathervane may display. The other five elements — *arms, letters,*

The six elements in one weathervane: finial; revolving motif, here a simple pennant; arms, shaped from S-scrolls with leaf and flower ornament; good bold cardinal letters; a suspended three-dimensional ram with gilded textured fleece as mount; curly-ended C-scrolling. The mount dominates. The vane, symbolising the area's staple industry, has probably been on the cupola of Halifax Piece Hall, West Yorkshire, since it opened in 1779.

scrolling, mount and *finial* — are mainly decorative and virtually optional.

The four *arms* projecting at right angles from the spindle may be straight and horizontal, angled or intricately curved. Their purpose, like that of the *letters* they carry (NSEW, equally variable in style), is to indicate the cardinal compass points, and they must be properly aligned. Occasionally other letters are substituted, such as GDTK ('God Damn The Kaiser') put up during the First World War at Dormansland, Surrey, and since replaced by GBTQ ('God Bless The Queen'). *Scrolling* or patterning, ornament for its own sake, may be added, usually where the arms and spindle intersect. A solid immovable *mount* may feature on the spindle, especially where it emerges from the roof. A spindle that projects above the motif may have a knob, acorn, crown or other shape of *finial*.

No one knows when the first weathervane was contrived or in what form. The earliest records, well before the birth of Christ, describe already sophisticated constructions, such as the Tower of the Winds in Athens. Above its octagonal base, each side of which still pictures the wind it faces, there was once an 8 foot (2.4 metre) bronze Triton. As he swung he confronted the breeze, his rod pointing above the face illustrating whichever wind was blowing. Other accounts from these centuries before Christ suggest that weathervanes were already connected to interior dials and various meteorological instruments.

3

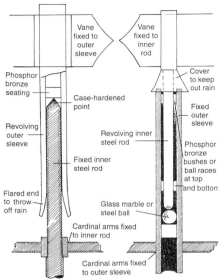

The two main methods by which vanes rotate: (left) motif attached to a tubular sleeve which drops over and rotates around a fixed spindle or rod; (right) motif attached to a solid spindle which drops into and rotates within a fixed tubular sleeve. Shading indicates non-moving parts.

In function and construction twentieth-century weathervanes remain essentially unchanged; weathervane makers have always performed essentially similar tasks.

Firstly, they *balance* the motif; ideally they provide roughly equal weights on either side of the spindle to reduce friction, but an appreciably larger tail area to swing the smaller pointer steadily into the wind.

Secondly, they make the motif *rotate* freely. One smith may choose to extend part of the motif sideways into rings which encircle the spindle like collars. Another may sharply point the spindle rod or terminate it with a depression cradling a ball bearing, over which a tube in the motif is slipped like a cap on a pen. Yet another may use a tubular sleeve and a motif with a solid spike that drops into it. Every smith favours his own method and derides all others. But very old examples survive to vouch for the effectiveness of all these methods.

Finally, every smith still strives to make his materials, his methods, the sizes and proportions of his motif and other elements all harmonise with each other and with the position the vane is to occupy. Nothing should seem arbitrary or extraneous.

Arms and scrolling have remained the preserve of wrought iron: development has primarily responded to changing tastes in style and materials for motifs. Most of these, until the mid nineteenth century, were cut from sheet iron or copper. Paint or gold leaf protected surfaces and enhanced the simplest shapes, which increasingly after about 1720 were embellished with pointers too. Skilled smiths could hammer sheet copper, either into moulds or freehand, to fashion, for example, in the sixteenth century the powerful three-dimensional Black Lion of Flanders, now on the Deryck Carver pub in Brighton, East Sussex, and in 1710 the splendid ship model now inside Portsmouth Cathedral, Hampshire. Swallow-

Cutting a silhouette vane from mild steel, using an oxyacetylene cutter. Once the metal has been scribed with the image, tiny drilled holes help the cutter to change direction but keep sharp angles. Rough edges will be filed and a protective coating applied. Blacksmith: Bill Cordaroy, East Ruston, Norfolk.

4

Casting motifs from a wooden or plaster pattern has two main advantages. A carved pattern highlights rounded forms, clarifies details and simulates textures as diverse as silk and bark. It can also be reproduced indefinitely. For limited numbers the pattern is pressed into sand to make a mould, which is then filled with molten metal (Jay's Foundry, Norwich). The thousands of Victorian cocks and banners, however, required more durable metal moulds.

tailed pennants were much in vogue in the eighteenth century. The Victorians moulded their plump cocks and ubiquitous small banners in cast iron. Today, swell-bodied forms may be moulded in aluminium or fibreglass, and flat motifs cut from steel, aluminium or plastics. Scenic or narrative vanes have been especially popular throughout the twentieth century: some department stores sell a coloured stage coach, forced to a halt before a menacing highwayman.

No matter how sound the materials and workmanship are, storms, vandals, atmospheric corrosives and mere age take their toll. Most weathervanes we see today, therefore, date from the eighteenth century onwards. At least two British church weathervanes, however, have survived for over six hundred years: a cock at Ottery St Mary, Devon, and a banner at Etchingham, East Sussex. Both illustrate how admirably weathervanes continue to perform a triple role, to *function*, to do so *decoratively*, and to convey *ideas* beyond themselves. The cock also belongs to the larger of the two weathervane 'families', the representational, while the banner represents the smaller family of heraldic and purely ornamental vanes.

Left: *Britain's oldest cock weathervane, c.1340, on the church at Ottery St Mary, Devon. Its gilded tail was renewed after Cromwellian musketry practice, but the wind humming through its unique breast tubes was not silenced until the twentieth century.*

Right: *Britain's oldest heraldic weathervane, c.1370, is of copper, pierced to represent 'azure a fret argent', the arms of Sir Thomas Echyngham, on Etchingham church, East Sussex. Compass indicators were often deemed unnecessary on churches.*

The early nineteenth-century artist John Sell Cotman designed the fine vane (left) at Knapton, Norfolk, with its double symbolism of the cock and saints' emblems. Strengthening rods, normally an eyesore, skilfully enhance the bird's strutting posture. The vane was restored at the nearby North Sea gas terminal. High-quality decorative ironwork is the priority in the stylised cock (right) at Bolney, West Sussex. It has required no maintenance beyond an occasional greasing since it was made in the 1930s.

THE TWO FAMILIES

Most people's immediate idea of a weathervane is a cock. This perennially popular image performs all three roles of a weathervane particularly well.

First, whether flat or three-dimensional, the function of wind indicating is admirably served by its smallish head and large flaunting tail.

Second, the cock is an inherently decorative subject. As it rotates its asymmetry creates everchanging effects. Each of its four main physical features — head, body, legs and tail — offers great freedom of interpretation in shape and posture, and their variety when combined is virtually limitless. Until quite recently the cock, though ubiquitous, was seldom exactly duplicated.

Third, especially on churches, whether portrayed realistically or stylised, it conveys certain messages. Its pagan association with the virility and power of the sun-god became transmuted into the Christian message of the power of the Church; associations with Peter's denial of Christ urged vigilance against sin. Secular interpretations came to focus on the swivelling of the cock as an image of fickleness.

Only rarely can the date of a cock weathervane be inferred from its appearance, because early stylised shapes continue into the present alongside increasingly realistic representations developed since the eighteenth century. Even an incised date may not refer to the cock itself so much as to the building or an event. And although a vane's history may be at one with its location, sometimes owners of mellow old farmhouses commission brand new weathervanes to suit, or builders incorporate venerable vanes into brash new developments.

As an easily identifiable image, the cock is the ancestor of all other representational and pictorial weathervanes.

The other obvious ancestor is the heraldic weathervane. Originally, on the battlefield, a coat of arms served to identify an individual. By the thirteenth and fourteenth centuries, when armorial devices, showily gilded or brilliantly coloured, were appearing on weathervanes, the display or decorative element clearly predominated. Heraldic vanes also implied by their shape the personal status achieved by the owner or his forebears. Simple triangular pennants bearing personal arms were the right of all knights. Pennants with swallow-tails (Lambeth Palace, London) denoted higher rank and some military achievement, while the square banner (Etchingham, East Sussex) rewarded those men, sometimes ennobled on the spot, whose success in battle was significant or spectacular.

Several factors led to the decline of heraldic weathervanes. Some authentic arms became so complex that only selected features could be presented on metal vanes, their mounts or finials. In later centuries lax heraldic control allowed people with little claim to rank and no authorisation to raise weathervanes with armorial-type designs that were little more than personal invention. Artisan blacksmiths, increasingly unfamiliar with the significance of heraldic devices, sometimes rendered them inaccurately — as did other artists: the famous Liver Bird, of which there is a good weathervane in Brighton, East Sussex, was intended as a heraldic eagle.

The obvious descendants of these heraldic ancestors were Victorian and Edwardian vanes. These employed heraldic banner

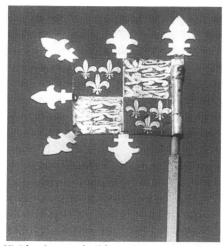

Vivid colour and gilding characterise all the vanes on Chichester market cross, West Sussex. Here the four quarterings of France and England represent Henry VII, ruler in 1501 when the cross was built. Weathervanes cannot cope with much greater armorial complexity than this.

(Left) As well as using a mitre finial, William Juxon, who became Archbishop of Canterbury in 1661, could have displayed his arms, impaled with those of the See of Canterbury, on a banner; the swallow-tailed pennant indicates his inherited military rank. On Lambeth Palace, London, the vane replicates the original destroyed in the Blitz. (Centre) A cock's head and neck are an amusing addition to a standard Victorian cast-iron banner at Knightwick, Worcestershire. The cardinal letters are also standard Victorian styles, but as each is from a different set more than the motif may have been tampered with. (Right) In 1913 councillors at Lowestoft, Suffolk, were horrified to discover that the rose-and-crown emblem used innocently on the town's arms since the seventeenth century had never been granted, so officially they had no right to this 1880s vane on the town hall. Economy has reduced the hollow rose with its sealed edges from gold leaf to yellow paint.

(Left) A modern vane, designed in traditional style for the new extension to Bury St Edmunds Cathedral, Suffolk, in 1960. Although appearing black in silhouette, it dazzles with gold leaf. (Centre) St Blaise, one of two saints raised on Guildford Old People's Centre, Surrey, for Queen Elizabeth II's Silver Jubilee. He carries his pastoral staff and the wool-comb by which he was martyred. The woolpack arrow-tail acknowledges one source of Guildford's prosperity. (Right) Almost overwhelmed by its decoration — deteriorating after forty years — this cut banner has as centrepiece the medical staff and serpent emblem, a suitable memorial to the former doctor owner at Waxham, Norfolk.

and pennant shapes but the success they proclaimed was industrial prosperity, the ability to afford prodigal decoration: a factory at Kirriemuir, Tayside, still flies over 120. Manufacturers were endlessly inventive in their treatment of solid shapes, cut designs and 'filigree' castings, sturdily made and carefully matched with other iron products such as railings. These vanes are often extremely attractive, even if they are period pieces which rarely catch the timeless grace of the truly heraldic vanes from which they derived.

Late twentieth-century designers still use these traditional banner and pennant shapes for decorative weathervanes with no heraldic significance. Occasionally, however, armorially correct vanes are still created, especially for new civic buildings. More interestingly, some genuinely heraldic older vanes are reinterpreted. For instance, the Victorians would have seen the fine weathervane on Halifax Town Hall, West Yorkshire, as the Paschal Lamb, derived from the eleventh-century military emblem

of the Knights Hospitallers. But future generations will understand this lamb-and-flag device to represent Yorkshire wool production, as it does according to the arms of Calderdale Metropolitan Borough.

Cocks and heraldic vanes are not alone in conveying messages. From them have developed weathervanes in many other shapes whose primary purpose is symbolic. On churches fish, doves, ships and evil dragons have obvious Christian connotations; wheels, gridirons and even arrows recall particular martyred saints. Britannia and the Union Flag, above Great Yarmouth pier, Norfolk, and Scarborough church, North Yorkshire, respectively, reflect patriotic fervour. Somewhat incongruously swinging a Norman soldier above Colchester Castle, Essex, is an internationally understood symbol, the yin-yang emblem of harmony.

Less grandly, a weathervane may allude to what goes on beneath it. So an elephant with his mahout identifies the former Indian Institute in Oxford, while at Pangbourne, Berkshire, games equipment indicates a

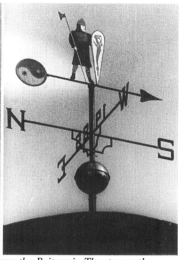

(Above left) Britannia, in copper with colour detail, suitably adorns the Britannia Theatre on the Britannia Pier at Great Yarmouth, Norfolk. (Above centre) Typically elaborate Victorian ornament almost overshadows the lamb-and-flag emblem in this substantial weathervane on Halifax Town Hall, West Yorkshire. Interpretations of the emblem have modified over the centuries. (Above right) This Norman soldier is appropriate for Colchester Castle, Essex, which is part Roman, part Norman. The yin-yang symbol in the glass tail of the vane is an internationally understood emblem of harmony and betrays the modern date, 1985. (Below left) A brightly coloured Union Flag provides patriotic embellishment for the church at Scarborough, North Yorkshire. (Bottom left) A somewhat unsubtle shape, but the neatly cut lines indicate clearly the range of activities available at this playing field alongside the Thames at Pangbourne, Berkshire. (Below right) Known as the 'Spirit of Lurgashall', this interesting vane was constructed by a resident of the village in West Sussex, in part from easily replaceable hardboard. The village green and its chestnut tree remain nearby although the geese and goose girl have gone.

playing field. A windmill vane is likely to mark the home of the Miller family or to recall how Mill Lane acquired its name. On the Royal Exchange in London the grasshopper emblem of its founder, Sir Thomas Gresham, has come to symbolise general mercantile activity. Ploughs, barrels, taps and assorted tools are more likely to be specific trade signs. Vanes depicting pub names, the promotional 'freezer-man' above Bejam's store in Hertford and the Lloyd's Bank prancing horse are all instantly recognisable, and permanent advertisements. Guitars, beehives and other objects whose significance may be puzzling probably symbolise hobbies or personal experiences.

Such symbolic vanes may become confusing when new businesses occupy the premises or families move on. For even in the late twentieth century we still subconsciously absorb the resonances as well as the physical appearance of a weathervane.

The Rose and Crown at Bainbridge, North Yorkshire, supplements its conventional innsign with a weathervane showing a rose and crown hanging in an oak tree, reminders of the flight of Charles II after the battle of Worcester in 1651.

(Left) An unequivocal message in the finial of this weathervane on the Mothercare store in a modern shopping precinct, Bury St Edmunds, Suffolk. In older parts of the town the vanes are more restrained. (Right) Two successful 'deliveries' have been made at Chwilog, Gwynedd. Each daughter has her name and date of arrival on one side of the vane, which their proud father made in 1986.

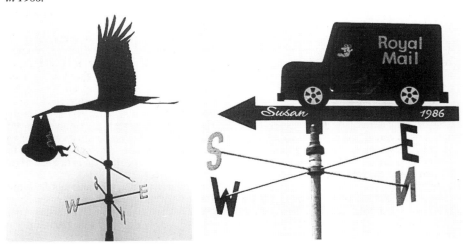

The charm of ducklings, creatures for which we feel more affection than for most farm products, is endearingly caught at Aldbourne, Wiltshire.

LIVING CREATURES

Creatures with obvious heads, bodies, often tails and usually legs to anchor them are potentially good weathervane shapes. Of wild creatures, birds are by far the most popular subject.

It is not easy to portray a bird in flight without apparently impaling it by wing or leg. So birds perched, alighting or rising — still in contact with something solid — are much preferred. From a spectacular ostrich at Strathdon, Grampian, and an osprey at Aviemore, Highland, many species are portrayed, right down to wrens. However, the depiction may not entirely succeed, especially when a vane is necessarily so much larger than a bird whose very diminutiveness is its charm. Most portrayals are naturalistic, but the characterful expressions of owls have been notably exploited in several designs in which the owls assume human postures, wearing mortar-boards or gossiping.

Most popular of all are game birds and wildfowl, probably because they are not simply representational but also signify a human activity connected with them. The favourite pheasant, at every conceivable level of accuracy, stands on grassy banks, holding its distinctive tail at many angles. At George Bernard Shaw's old home at Ayot St Lawrence, Hertfordshire, the three-dimensional bird not only swings to the wind's direction but raises and lowers its laterally hollowed tail as the wind varies in strength.

Partridges, geese and ducks are also favoured images. But it is the shooting of game birds that is the great attraction, and whole shooting scenes abound. If a bird occurs in such scenes at all it will be a pheasant, but usually the quarry is implied, and the scene concentrates on the human figure, aiming or waiting with his dog. Portraits of particular men with particular dogs, or an emphasis on landscape, confirm that in these vanes the interest is in the activity, not the birds.

Similarly, among wild animals those most frequently adopted as weathervanes are creatures of the chase — stags, hares, boars, and above all the wily but grudgingly respected fox. Fox vanes are everywhere, in

(Left) In curlew country at Dallowgill, near Leyburn, North Yorkshire, this farm vane is typical in its use of available and redundant materials: old hearth tongs form the arrow. (Right) Variations on this vane at Ide Hill, Kent, were popular in the 1920s. The exact size and placing of the eyes establishes the character of the birds, here pleasingly perched on a branch, not a rod.

town and country, in three dimensions or silhouette, in coats of many colours. The symbolic element in the choice is clear when fox vanes surmount stables full of hunters or the country homes of hunt members. But many fox vanes postdate hunting's heyday. Indeed, contemporary blacksmiths confirm that the fox design is one of the favourites from the Rural Development Commission's pattern book. On private homes the fox seems to hint at nostalgia for the old stability of country life in times of rapid technological change and perhaps an aspiration towards the activities and status of the big house.

While sometimes the weathervane fox chases a cock or goose, more often he is himself at full stretch, fleeing his pursuers. Hunting scenes are legion. The fox, followed by several hounds and huntsman, lopes in leisurely style or races frenetically across the sky. In a popular design on the Royal Estate at Sandringham, Norfolk, the fox has escaped, and huntsman and hounds pace homewards. On a farm vane at Aldbrough St John, North Yorkshire, this huntsman becomes 'Jorrocks', overweight and underskilled as in R.S. Surtees's book, on a reluctant steed. A unique hunt scene at Capel, Kent, shares fox, hounds and hunts-

(Left) In full shooting scenes such as the one on this downwind-pointing vane near Hungerford, Berkshire, the disproportion between animals, sportsman and landscape often raises a smile. (Right) A lively pictorial shooting scene at Eynsford, Kent, is probably a 1930s design but is still being made. A variation shows the man unprepared, with the gun still on his shoulder.

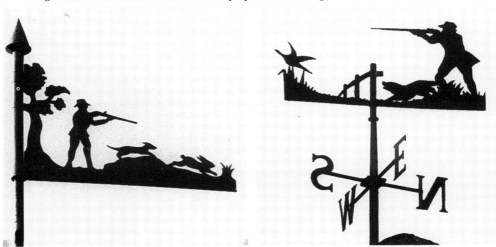

(Left) The deliberately inadequate figure of the stout huntsman 'Jorrocks' at Aldbrough St John, North Yorkshire, chases a contrastingly sophisticated slinking fox. (Right) Made from sugar-beet fork tines and other farm scrap, this farm vane at Weston Longville, Norfolk, was then sand-blasted and galvanised to be completely maintenance-free.

men among the bonnet tails of several separate oast-houses, so that the whole hunt comes realistically into view by stages as one passes.

Apart from creatures of the chase, other small British wild animals tend to be disregarded. Especially in the nineteenth century, it was exotic creatures that caught the imagination: lions, elephants and camels were thought far more interesting, both in life and as weathervane subjects.

No such dismissive attitude hindered the portrayal of domesticated animals, however. A persistent tradition of farmers knocking up their own vanes from farm oddments must be held responsible for the often comically stiff cattle, sheep, pigs and poultry that plod lifelessly above so many barns. But they function: they tell their owners when not to spray a particular field. And, pierced or painted to define a turkey (Shalford Green, Essex) or a Hereford bull

A hunt scene at Garforth, West Yorkshire, of typical design but painted with considerable skill, and ornamented with interesting horizontal scrolls.

(Left) A lively example, at Mattishall, Norfolk, of how exaggeration can sometimes catch the essence of a creature better than a more faithful likeness. (Right) Swell-bodied copper animals were among the most popular of the nineteenth-century American designs, frequently reproduced there and now sometimes in Britain too. The style of sphere and lettering is typical. This one is at Bembridge, Isle of Wight.

(Boughrood, Powys), they acknowledge what brings in the farm income.

Dogs of every kind join the sporting breeds and hounds of the hunting scenes as a weathervane subject. Cats and other pets appear too, but it is mainly dogs that are immortalised by fond owners. Technically uninspired some of these vanes may be, but devoted mutual relationships come through with touching clarity.

Horses, too, have a special relationship with those who own or care for them. Until Eadweard Muybridge was able to demonstrate with his 'zoopraxiscope' in the 1870s precisely how a horse's leg movements followed each other, depicting them accurately was a matter of luck. But the horse's combination of grace and solidity has long challenged, and sometimes defeated, weathervane makers. As with so many subjects, if a particular horse and attitude can be imagined, it has probably, expertly or ineptly, been reproduced as a weathervane. And since the horse's relationship with man is paramount, especially in racing centres like Newmarket, Suffolk, it is often a horse mounted by a rider, being urged over a gate, racing past a winning post or pulling a carriage that is shown. Again, nostalgia or aspiration can be seen at work.

The ideal natural form, a sleek fish with vertical tail-fin, offers so little wind resistance that some fish vanes are probably older than we realise. At one extreme are simplified cigar shapes; at the other, species identifiable by their accurate fins, gills, scales and simulated movement. Perhaps such comic humanised dolphins as that at Worlington, Suffolk, derive from heraldic representation, but sharks, a whale at Beaulieu, Hampshire, even a sea-horse at Writtle, Essex, preserve something of their natural dignity. Fish vanes on churches at Torver (Cumbria), Crimond (Grampian) and elsewhere perpetuate a scholarly sym-

The racing colours of Lord Carnarvon are identifiable on this rapidly deteriorating vane at Upper Lambourn, Berkshire; the name of the horse is not recorded.

14

bolism: the initial letters of the Greek words for 'Jesus Christ, God's Son, Saviour' spell out the Greek word for 'fish'. On private dwellings recognisable salmon and trout, and even pike, seem like lucky charms for keen anglers.

Fish are usually presented alone, and rarely swimming through water. When the human element is introduced, illustrating fly or coarse fishing, longshore or sea angling, operating from land or boat, the proverbial fishermen's yarns are often pictured, in scenes of epic struggle between mere mortals and monsters of the deep.

Botanical subjects are difficult to reproduce. Trees can be successfully portrayed but smaller plants, even sturdy tulips at Moulton, Lincolnshire, may look thickset and clumsy. A butterfly rests fleetingly at Hickling, Norfolk, but bees, as at Hatching Green, Hertfordshire, and Mytholmroyd, West Yorkshire, become menacing at weathervane size. Frogs and toads are usually treated as figures of fun.

(Top left) The accuracy of this bass at Trebetherick, Cornwall, is guaranteed by its owner, an international authority on the species. An unconventional asymmetrical mounting increases the vane's efficiency. (Top right) Typically, the fish is big enough to swamp the boat in this jolly fishing scene by the river at Brundall, Norfolk. (Lower left) The active gaiety of this frog at Bromham, Wiltshire, is conveyed by his tenuous foothold, which, however, leaves him very vulnerable to fierce winds. (Lower right) An unexpectedly wasp-waisted bee — on an apiary at Hatching Green, Hertfordshire.

15

(Above left) This energetic golfing figure on a vane at Southwold, Suffolk is claimed to be Nick Faldo. (Above right) By contrast, in Merseyside, the Royal Birkdale Golf Club's player and caddie, probably erected when plus-fours were the height of golfing fashion, are unexpectedly static. (Below left) A pigeon-fancier commissioned this appropriate vane for his home in Chingford, London. These cardinal arms, created from scrolls, are the distinctive style of a particular blacksmith. (Below right) Two sports on one vane are unusual, but a public bowling green and tennis courts flank this vane on a park pavilion in Worthing, West Sussex. The curvaceous lettering suggests a 1920s origin.

Overweight and underpowered they may be, but this is a neat compact rowing four, made by a former oarsman west of Cambridge to replace whatever motif originally topped these mass-produced cardinal arms.

AT LEISURE AND WORK

The riding, hunting, shooting and fishing weathervanes already mentioned illustrate some people's leisure activities, but many other pursuits — athletics, team games such as football, rugby and hockey, and more individual sports — are also weathervane subjects. With its constant modification to sportswear and equipment, sport is essentially up-to-the-minute. So a weathervane picturing a golfer in baggy plus-fours (Royal Birkdale Golf Club, Southport, Merseyside) or a tennis player with an oddly proportioned racquet (Falmouth, Cornwall) is likely to date from when such items were the newest thing and thus acquires some historical interest. Unfortunately, vanes of this kind tend not to be replicated or preserved but replaced with more up-to-date equivalents.

Teams of eleven or fifteen players, in which the whole team is the unit, are not easy subjects. There are few footballing vanes. The Rugby Football Union ground at Twickenham, Middlesex, shows two players, but one has winged feet, portraying Hermes.

More suitable subjects for weathervanes are sports with teams compactly grouped, such as the rowing eight on Fen Ditton church, Cambridgeshire, or performed by players one at a time, as in cricket. One of many vigorously posed batsmen performs by Brentor Cricket Club pavilion, Devon. Stumps, bat and ball may appear not only with a player but sometimes on their own — a feature shared by golfing equipment, sailing dinghies, hot air balloons and so on.

Sports relying chiefly on solo performances such as golf, bowls, tennis and the more esoteric motocross, mountaineering, boxing, falconry or skating are probably rendered into weathervanes because of the sporting predilection of the owners. The addictive nature of golf, in particular, is reflected in the frequency with which every aspect of the game occurs on vanes. Some are unintentionally amusing: players adopt physically impossible attitudes, while at Hough-on-the-Hill, Lincolnshire, the head of the club is on the wrong side of the shaft. However, the likeness of Nick Faldo is claimed along Mill Street, Southwold, Suffolk; any particularly idiosyncratic stance probably pictures the owner himself or some international player he dreams of emulating. Alderley Edge Golf Club, Cheshire,

17

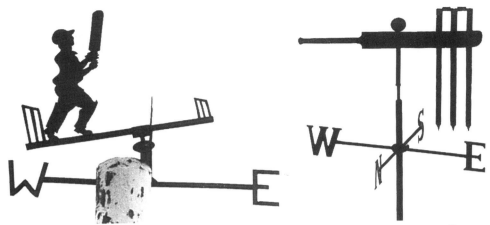

(Left) An energetic player and an interesting attempt to convey perspective on a mast at Brentor cricket club, Devon. The lettering, though clear, could be more stylish. (Right) A simple bold arrangement of cricket equipment at Stonegate, East Sussex.

has one of several groups of golfers, in characteristic attitudes, with their equipment.

While golfing weathervanes are popular private choices, bowls club pavilions are the usual sites for bowls vanes. The moment of releasing the wood is almost the only pose, with an occasional onlooking opponent. Most are accurate, if not especially lively: a few show players sagging weakly at the knees.

Nearly all the weathervanes that illustrate cycling depict penny-farthings, so it seems that it is not the sporting activity that

is significant here but nostalgia and the machine's intriguing appearance. Similarly, purposeful walkers in boots and backpacks are rare. Their place is taken by pedestrians, male and female, old and young, in period or modern dress, all battling against a gale that blows umbrellas and dogs' ears inside out. Most raise a smile, including the Rural Development Commission's popular version. Leaning figures like those of two men with umbrellas at Barnham Broom, Norfolk, add strong diagonals to a design, as do the running children on Eynsford school, Kent.

(Left) A farmer at Barnham Broom, Norfolk, created this dramatically energetic group of windswept figures on his barn. (Right) At Chattisham, Suffolk, this penny-farthing, little more than a handspan in height, is a three-dimensional model, with each wheelspoke accurately inserted and the two-legged rider sitting astride and holding crosswise handlebars with his two arms.

Left: *This rare interior scene at Howe, Norfolk, is an amusing sight in lashing rain or a blizzard. One particular firm uses this pierced fishtail lettering.*

Right: *Former forges frequently mount blacksmiths at work. This one above a forge/garage near Skipton, North Yorkshire, has an interesting array of tools beside the anvil.*

Amidst such vigour we smile at the white-flannelled sportsman resting from his exertions in a tree-shaded deck-chair at Coddenham, Suffolk. And what could be more defiantly inactive than the rare contemporary scene of a man relaxing with pipe, slippers and cat in front of a television set (Howe, Norfolk)?

Considering how keenly most people concentrate on their leisure activities, it is perhaps surprising how many of them choose vanes depicting gainful employment. It is seldom their own employment, however.

Pictorial work vanes (as distinct from those on which tools symbolise a trade) largely illustrate the older, mainly rural tasks, which those who never had to do them in all weathers are prone to sentimentalise. So, the Rural Development Commission's ploughmen stroll effortlessly behind immaculate horses; their shepherds still wear smocks and dally in flowery woodland. For millers and stockmen, horse trainers, dairymaids and even poachers, time has similarly stood still. Blacksmiths have fared better: the firebox, bellows, anvil and tools, and the

(Left) Cast in aluminium, this tiny shepherding scene at Oving, Buckinghamshire, includes all the delicate foliage of the Rural Development Commission's original design, often omitted as too costly in versions cut from sheet metal. (Right) This pre-war vane depicting ploughman and horse at Arnesby, Leicestershire, was also designed by the Rural Development Commission. Such ploughmen are ubiquitous, though not always well executed, and are often painted.

(Left) This Artilleryman on the United Services Club, Whitehall, London, is too small to be seen clearly from the ground but the action of the scene and the way the vane is painted are to be admired. (Right) The nurse shaking her thermometer at a patient shrinking in bed on this weathervane on the hospital at Teddington, Middlesex, also requires binoculars to be appreciated.

way blacksmiths operate, have changed little. And as blacksmiths still make most weathervanes, their images of their own calling are predictably more accurate and less glamorised.

Although ploughing teams and shepherds are incongruous on modern housing estates, town dwellers seem reluctant to erect vanes showing urban or modern occupations. Carters, lamplighters, sedan chairmen and bargees would find few vacancies advertised today. The artilleryman and rifleman pictured above Whitehall, London, and in Haddenham, Buckinghamshire, would be at a loss in the modern army. The nurse above Teddington Hospital, Middlesex and the film-maker at Faversham, Kent, are archaically dressed and equipped. Education is poorly — if amusingly — served by manic mortar-boarded schoolmasters pursuing their taunting pupils, or by geography being taught from a globe revolving horizontally — both designs almost exclusive to schools! The most successful up-to-date presentations are of firemen, various builders, bricklayers and carpenters, and gardeners (the Gardeners' Royal Benevolent Society logo originated as the weathervane on their retirement home at Henfield, West Sussex). The beekeeper's costume, above Beehive Cottage, Dunwich, Suffolk, is timeless. So is a delightfully detailed, if cynically imagined clergyman, ignoring his hourglass and preaching energetically to pews empty even of hymn-books. The clue to the vane's age is its location: almost certainly Edwin Lutyens himself created it for a house he designed in 1901 in Sonning, Berkshire.

The archaic air of these occupational vanes is in itself partly symbolic — of a general yearning for a past when life appeared more stable and employment more satisfying. As they rarely relate to the occupation of the owner they seem to fulfil the desire for charm rather than relevance. But it is always worth checking the location of an occupational vane. A blacksmith on the Old Forge, a pieman on the Old Bakehouse, a milkmaid on Dairy Cottage are pointing us towards a snippet of social history.

Vanes of this type, all similar but not identical, are favoured on schools or former school buildings. The running children are often cribbed from the old school road sign. This is at Noke, Oxfordshire.

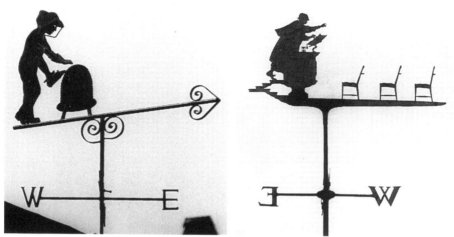

(Left) An unusual subject, but appropriate on Beehive Cottage, near Dunwich, Suffolk. The pleasingly lifelike beekeeper is well equipped with veil, gloves and smoker to control the bees in his hive. (Right) Edwin Lutyens probably designed this vane at Sonning, Berkshire, remarkable for its refined detail. The preaching clergyman is quite unabashed by his lack of congregation.

A popular vane on schools since the early twentieth century and as a gift for retiring teachers, this geography lesson is nonetheless inaccurate — the globe's axis is wrong. A gaily painted example from Brayford, Devon.

21

Above left: *Delightful detail in this buggy vane at Croscombe, Somerset, is enhanced by lines of perforations. The motif is rather awkwardly mounted, however.*

Right: *Stephenson's 'Rocket', thought to have been placed on the Municipal Buildings, Crewe, Cheshire, about 1900, is a small but elegant 'model', of a type familiar in nineteenth-century America but rare in Britain.*

Below left: *Its size, lofty mounting and dramatic outline make this a most effective farm vane at Hindringham, Norfolk.*

Above right: *The 'George V' engine and tender, in silhouette but with a good deal of correctly painted detail, above an enthusiast's home at Winson, Gloucestershire.*

Below right: *An enduring favourite from the Rural Development Commission's range. Enthusiasts paint it as fancy dictates — here at Barroway Drove, Norfolk, it is bright yellow and black and clearly detailed — and claim it as an Austin, Morris, Renault, etcetera.*

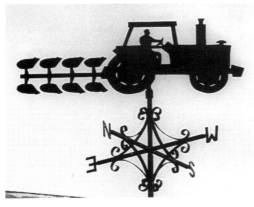

The detail achievable by the casting process can be readily appreciated at close quarters, so such a vane is best mounted on a low building. This is one of Brandeston Forge's popular designs.

VEHICLES AND VESSELS

Weathervanes illustrate all the chief means of propulsion from the horse to Concorde. Horse-drawn vehicles are particularly popular subjects. Weathervanes show donkey traps, mail and stage coaches, small smart gigs and the sort of carriages that are driven for sport, often dashing along drawn by the appropriate number of animals. Even if they run to such details as wheel-spokes, they are almost all cut in silhouette; a few, like the cast design from Brandeston Forge, Suffolk, show contrasting textures.

It is steam engines that apparently fire weathervane makers with the greatest enthusiasm. All sorts of traction engines appear. Many represent machines, still lovingly preserved, that ploughed and threshed on the farm. Cranmer House, Fakenham, Norfolk, displays a 1903 Burrell engine, accurate to the manufacturer's catalogue. Within the constraints of silhouette presentation, many engines are so faithfully reproduced that experts can identify the precise model intended. The same is true of portable fairground engines and named steam locomotives. Extremely intricate three-dimensional locomotives, virtually to scale models, were cast in America during its late nineteenth-century weathervane heyday. Theoretically the moulds could still be used, but their complexity demands so many separate processes that the cost would be prohibitive. Stephenson's *Rocket*, on Crewe Municipal Buildings, Cheshire, is in this style, but its origin is unknown.

When tractors, powered by internal combustion engines, took to the fields, farm workers became as fond of them as of the horses they had replaced, and early tractors are popular subjects on rural weathervanes. Pride in more modern machines is less evident, though an early combine harvester vane at Rockland St Peter, Norfolk, has reappeared elsewhere.

It is difficult to understand why the car has produced relatively few weathervanes. There are some baby Austins, some 1920s Bentley tourers, even the occasional post-war Jaguar, with windows cut out or painted. On homes these chiefly indicate old favourites of private owners; on service stations, a manufacturer's agency. Now that aerodynamic shaping has drastically reduced the distinction between various makes of car, and driving has become more of a necessity than a pleasure, modern cars, like

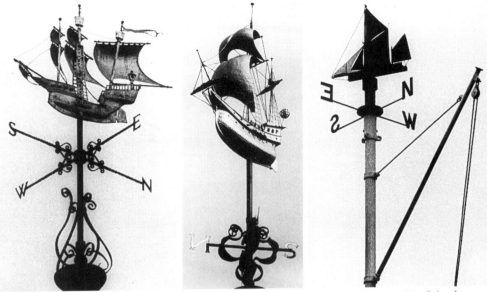

(Left) This three-dimensional gilt sailing ship, possibly the 'Good Hope', on Ogilvie School at Clacton, Essex, is decorative rather than accurate. (Centre) Intricate rigging and the beacon-light 'basket' astern enhance this fine gilded three-dimensional Tudor vessel — appropriate on Lloyd's Register of Shipping, London. Its pivot point and sail arrangement make it 'sail' downwind. (Right) Distance from the sea is no deterrent. This attractively painted masthead barge is at Leek, Staffordshire, evidence of the wide popularity of ship weathervanes.

modern trains and buses, do not inspire weathervane makers.

Ships, however, especially sailing vessels, exert an immense fascination. Yet a sailing-ship vane is even more of a compromise and illusion than most designs — no vessel, with sails set and trimmed, can point anything like directly into the wind, as it has to on a weathervane.

Three-dimensional square-rigged ships, looking like scale models, are at once the most illusionistic, the most spectacular and the most vulnerable to heavy weather. Real ships were designed to catch as much of the wind in their sails as possible — exactly the opposite requirement to a ship on a vane, which the wind should preferably slip past without damage. Moreover, even with only some of its sails set and drawing, a ship weathervane not only endures tremendous lateral pressure but will swing away from the wind, not towards it. This may not matter when the vane becomes familiar but a quick glance at, for instance, the ship

above Lloyd's Register of Shipping in London, can be confusing. The compromise of showing square sails furled and only the fore-and-aft mizzen set at the stern is both clearer and safer; the mizzen swings the weathervane ship to face the wind, just as it would if she were at anchor.

Rigging such ships accurately is an increasing mystery to modern sailors, let alone blacksmiths. But the fact that the attractive ship on Ogilvie School, Clacton, Essex, is only one of those with sails blowing one way and masthead pennants the other suggests that, even in supposed ship portraits, decorativeness has taken precedence over likelihood, and even over efficiency.

Three-dimensional 'model' vanes have always been costly. Beautiful medieval cogs, Tudor galleons and windjammers are therefore restricted mainly to public buildings or aristocratic homes such as York Cottage, Sandringham, Norfolk. Luckily a few highly skilled craftsmen can still make them: Cabot's flagship at Bristol, Avon, and *Mary Rose* at Farnham, Surrey, are two modern examples.

Although not second-rate, silhouette ship vanes are made for private home rather than for civic buildings and so their quality is more variable. Again there is an enormous historical and geographical range. The cogs, fourmasters and schooners reappear as silhouettes. So do Chinese junks, Mediterranean war galleys, Viking longships and trading barges as well as modern cruising and racing yachts, fishing boats and dinghies. Usually, any craft peculiar to a region will predominate in local weathervanes. Even on churches, where they express the general idea of the Church as a safe vessel for life's journey, these regional craft often feature. So Nefyn church, Gwynedd, for instance, depicts the kind of clipper built there, while Southwold church, Suffolk, shows an east-coast sail drifter.

Sail drifters became steam drifters, and it is these that make the only sizeable group of powered craft to appear on weathervanes. Because they are frequently made by retired fishermen for their own homes, they are often minutely accurate. The very few warships seem to belong to ex-naval men. Overall, it is clear that as a genre ships of all kinds join cocks and foxes as the most enduring weathervane subjects.

Whether the same will be true of aeroplanes is uncertain, especially if the engineers continue to design out differences in appearance. Blériot's plane on a mansion

Blériot's plane of 1909 is unexpected in Troutbeck, above Windermere, Cumbria. The complex hollow sphere beneath almost suggests the world, the spanning of which by flight suddenly seemed a possibility.

overlooking Windermere is an early rarity. Fokkers, Dakotas and Spitfires have all been identified. But since Jet Range helicopters and Concorde are also depicted, perhaps this is the one mode of transport in which it is the excitement of the newest developments that fires weathervane makers.

(Left) At Stutton, Suffolk, above ready-made cardinal arms a commissioned motif — the Lowestoft herring drifter 'Lydia Eva', now part of the Maritime Museum collection — was used as a project for patients at a nearby mental hospital. (Centre) One of the Rural Development Commission's designs, the sailing dinghy is detailed enough without being cluttered. An inward-turned E usually implies that a vane is viewed primarily from the north side. (Right) Whatever the original significance of 1961 for this household in Haywards Heath, West Sussex, the clever arrangement of the figures to read equally well from either side continues to give pleasure by its ingenuity and decorativeness.

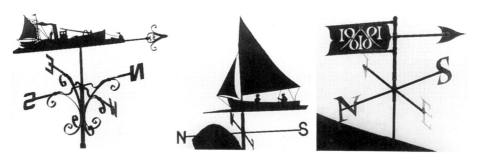

(Above left) The accession of Queen Anne — Anna Regina — is recorded on a church in Rye, East Sussex. The scrolling is perhaps over-elaborate. (Above right) The obelisk in the market place at Ripon, North Yorkshire, is surmounted by this locally manufactured vane showing the Wakeman's horn, used to set the watch and still sounded nightly. The mount is a rowel spur. (Below left) A clergyman erected this vane at Whiston, Northamptonshire, showing Gladstone at the mercy of the British lion. (Below right) This gallant charging Wellington is to be found on a block of modern flats in Waterloo Place, Lewes, East Sussex.

(Left) The large statue of the local hero John Hampden in the market place, Aylesbury, Bucking-hamshire, is the source for the figure on this weathervane on the new golf centre near Bierton. (Right) 'One of the Barons Ogle (later Dukes of Newcastle) hunting deer in his park', recorded the designer. He also substituted for cardinal arms a three-dimensional thistle to point north to Scotland and a rose south to England, in this border area of Ogle, Northumberland.

FACT AND FICTION

Eyecatching weathervanes, responding to the wind and cut decoratively with dates or initials, can serve to remind us of events and people of importance, at both national and local level. Coronations and jubilees, the restoration of the village church and its benefactor, births and marriages — all can be commemorated, and if the events and individuals are difficult to identify after a while it does not matter, for these vanes are primarily a contemporary celebration. For this reason dated weathervanes are notoriously deceptive; later generations may choose to replicate an old worn vane, but equally they may prefer to record the date of something quite different.

Pictorial symbols, therefore, like the pilgrim ship on Hingham church, Norfolk, or the Wakeman's Horn at Ripon, North Yorkshire, not only have more visual impact than dates but also recall their source of inspiration more readily.

Many historical characters are identifiable. Rulers such as Boudicca and Henry VIII have been portrayed, war heroes like Wellington and Nelson, politicians like Gladstone. Other figures, although not nationally renowned, are likely to be familiar within more limited circles: the founder of a firm to its employees and clients; a former Principal on Loughborough College of Technology, Leicestershire; a notable resident or titled landowner. Figures such as the Roman centurion at Hedenham, Norfolk, and the crusader at Meriden, West Midlands, are assumed to make some reference to the area's history.

Whoever is portrayed, from whatever period, a vane showing a human figure is unlikely to be much over 120 years old. Before that the human form was seldom used on weathervanes, and then it usually portrayed 'Wisdom' or 'Industry', not a named individual. The step from an ab-

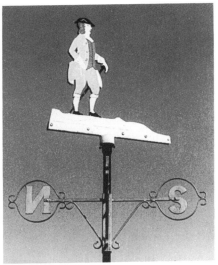

A London firm founded in 1780 by George Jackson and the Adam brothers still creates architectural embellishments for quality buildings. George Jackson's smart and colourful wooden figure surveys Bosham Harbour, West Sussex, from the boathouse of a former managing director. The letter mounts are unusual.

stract 'Faith' to a named person exemplifying that quality was not great, however, and figures of St George, St Michael, St Francis and other saints are scattered about the land. Usually they adorn religious buildings, but St Bryce makes a fine modern weathervane on the Town House at Kirkcaldy, Fife.

From saints, it was a small step to angels and archangels, of whom the most spectacular must be the 15 foot (4.6 metre) high, 1 ton three-dimensional gilded angel with dramatically outflung arm above Guildford Cathedral, Surrey.

In direct contrast to angels, dragons are often seen as the embodiment of evil — and thus endlessly fascinating. On churches they are sometimes said to show that in the building beneath sinners will be saved from the jaws of hell. However, dragon vanes also have heraldic origins: under the outstretched wings of Wren's famous dragon on Bow church, London, for instance, are red crosses, as on the dragon supporters of the City's coat of arms. In Wessex and Wales dragons arouse fierce regional loyalties. In all their manifestations dragons are abundantly decorative. Sixteenth-century craftsmen produced the three-dimensional

(Left) St Francis feeds the birds at Ditchling, East Sussex, in a clear evocation of the Giotto fresco in Assisi. The position of the pivot point so far aft suggests that the pointer may have had too little weight. (Right) A change of dedication from St Michael to St Peter in 1220 entitles both saints, with sword and key respectively, to surmount the church at Thundersley, Essex. The figures are too equally balanced, but with the additional arrow the vane indicates more accurately.

(Left) This lively, toothy dragon is at Orleton church, Worcestershire, which is dedicated to St George. (Centre) This three-dimensional gilded angel on the cathedral at Guildford, Surrey, may be the largest British vane. The angel is 15 feet (4.6 metres) tall and weighs a ton. The fierce attitude provides a fitting challenge to the menacing dragons also popular on churches, such as the one at Harlow New Town, Essex (right). The initials JA on the Harlow vane are those of a beneficent local landowner at the date indicated. The dragon would probably then have been regarded with greater awe than it evokes in the present inhabitants.

one in gilded copper on Newark Park, Gloucestershire, now owned by the National Trust. The Victorians' favourite, cast in quantity, is still especially numerous in seaside resorts, splendidly sinuous and scaly-winged.

Story-tellers and writers have invented all sorts of other fabulous beasts and supernatural beings over the centuries, to astound, reassure or influence their audiences. Among twentieth-century renderings that bear witness to their continuing appeal are a griffin (Forfar church, Tayside), a mermaid (Hoddesdon, Hertfordshire), a unicorn (Bisley, Gloucestershire), a phoenix (Chester city wall), Pegasus (Foston Hall prison, Derbyshire) and Santa Claus (Aviemore, Highland). Father Time at Lord's Cricket Ground, London, so apparently timeless, dates only from 1925; he is now cheaply mass-produced and private makers are interpreting the idea with considerable freedom.

Sixteenth-century crafts-men made this forceful dragon of beaten copper, still substantially original, on Newark Park, Ozleworth, Gloucestershire, a National Trust property. A lightning strike was almost fortuitous, since the restoration included regilding.

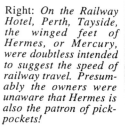

Left: *Half man, half horse, the centaur stands impressively, if unexpectedly, on High Wycombe Guildhall, Buckinghamshire. His tail has been lengthened to make him a more efficient wind indicator.*

Right: *On the Railway Hotel, Perth, Tayside, the winged feet of Hermes, or Mercury, were doubtless intended to suggest the speed of railway travel. Presumably the owners were unaware that Hermes is also the patron of pickpockets!*

Folk heroes, such as Robin Hood, and characters from nursery rhymes and fairy-tales seem to touch a similar chord. The most frequently seen on weathervanes are witches. Like the popularity of dragons, this seems to say something about how we relish visualising and confronting our terrors. In appearance, witches range from the benign to the demented, the most generally satisfying being the design from the Rural Development Commission; in execution they range from the sketchiest cut-outs to Brandeston Forge's carefully moulded example on which the cat's fur and broomstick bristles are sharply delineated.

Weathervanes depicting characters from favourite children's books are almost always special commissions. Peter Pan is on St Christopher's School at Langford, Oxfordshire and Alice on Daresbury School, Cheshire, and Christopher Robin is on a house in Ivinghoe, Buckinghamshire.

The point about weathervanes like these is that the observer recognises the character and recalls the rest of the story. There are some, however, whose background is familiar only to those with particular historical and cultural awareness. So workers

in London's Royal Exchange will realise that its grasshopper weathervane recalls the fabled rescue by these insects of its founder, Sir Thomas Gresham. Residents of Bungay, Suffolk will recognise on their town-centre weathervane the devilish hound Black Shuck, which slew men at prayer as it rampaged through their church. The crude fiddle vane at Great Ponton, Lincolnshire, reminds villagers of a poor itinerant fiddler who used the fortune he made in America to beautify the church for the villagers who had once helped him.

A surer way of communicating a story is to illustrate its key moment. Nonetheless, it will still be mainly the inhabitants of the Durham area who understand that the vane in the centre of Lambton (now part of Washington, Tyne and Wear) shows not just another George and Dragon but the Lambton Worm, bleeding to death under the spikes of John Lambton's armour. In Dorset, the eighteenth-century tale of the Shapwick Monster — a crab so huge and so incomprehensible to the farm labourers that they fled in terror — is entertainingly illustrated on Crab Farm, Shapwick. One local story, however, originating near Watton,

(Left) Many households flout the superstition that witches on chimneys bring bad luck. At Gwalchmai, Anglesey, Gwynedd, the exuberantly cackling witch devised by the Rural Development Commission, usually bare-headed, has acquired a hat. (Centre) The Marylebone Cricket Club's famous Father Time weathervane at Lord's Cricket Ground in London has weary dignity, but in this home-produced variation at Deeping St James, Lincolnshire, he creeps up on his victims with unholy glee. (Right) 'The Shapwick Monster' — a 1706 Dorset tale, illustrated on Crab Farm, Shapwick, Dorset. Although an older vane had at least one more figure, more characterful faces and more finely detailed farm implements, this is nonetheless an important record of a local legend and is maintained by the National Trust.

Norfolk, has become almost a national folk tale. A Watton vane shows the Babes cowering in the Wood while the two hired ruffians fight. The robin waits to cover their bodies, the first leaf already in his bill.

How different these vanes incorporating whole stories are from the cock, the simple square banner, the stolid cow, the golfer, the racing yacht... Yet the principles throughout remain constant. The weathervane maker seeks first to produce something that works efficiently. He will try to make it well. If it can also be attractive to look at, communicate an idea and arouse a response, then both the man who makes it and we who see it will find it pleasurable and satisfying.

Characters from popular children's stories. (Left) Peter Pan, on a school at Langford, Oxfordshire, is sometimes erroneously called the Pied Piper. He is, however, based on the statue of J. M. Barrie's famous character in Kensington Gardens. (Centre) Christopher Robin is shown contentedly fishing on this weathervane at Ivinghoe, Buckinghamshire. The ironwork is somewhat flimsy, but the maker has since produced more robust work. (Right) Two robbers fight while the Babes in the Wood cower in the undergrowth on this depiction of the fairytale at Watton, Norfolk, one of a series on old people's homes in the county. The story traditionally took place locally.

FURTHER READING

Bishop, Robert, and Coblentz, Patricia. *A Gallery of American Weathervanes and Whirli-gigs.* Bonanza Books, New York, 1981.
Chapman, Brigid. *The Weathervanes of Sussex.* Temple House Books, Lewes, 1987.
Fitzgerald, Ken. *Weathervanes and Whirligigs.* Clarkson N. Potter, New York, 1967.
Kaye, Myrna. *Yankee Weathervanes.* E.P. Dutton & Co, New York, 1975.
Klamkin, Charles. *Weathervanes: The History, Manufacture and Design of an American Folk Art.* Hawthorn Books, New York, 1973.
Messent, Claude. *The Weathervanes of Norfolk and Norwich.* Fletcher & Son, Norwich, 1937.
Mockridge, Patricia and Philip. *Weathervanes of Great Britain.* Robert Hale, London, 1990.
Needham, Albert. *English Weathervanes.* Charles Clarke, Haywards Heath, 1953.
Pagdin, W. E. *The Story of the Weathercock.* Edward Appleby Ltd, Stockton on Tees, 1949.

PLACES TO VISIT

Unlike the USA, where most weathervanes are housed indoors in museums and collections, the best place to see weathervanes in Britain is *in situ.* Look on every conceivable building, from church to garden shed, town hall to public lavatory, stately home to fish-curing factory, pierhead dance-hall to cemetery gatehouse. Some fragile examples may be inside churches rather than on them, and provincial museums sometimes display one of local interest. There is more than one weathervane in the following collections, but it is best to enquire whether they are on show before making a special journey.

The American Museum in Britain, Claverton Manor, Bath, Somerset BA2 7BD. Telephone: 01225 460503.
British Folk Art Collection, Countess of Huntingdon Chapel, The Vineyard, Paragon, Bath, Somerset BA1 5NA. Telephone: 01225 446020.
St Peter Hungate Church Museum, Princes Street, Norwich, Norfolk NR3 1AE. Telephone: 01603 667231.
The Victoria and Albert Museum, Cromwell Road, South Kensington, London SW7 2RL. Telephone: 0171-938 8500.

(Left) This stylised brass dolphin at Worlington, Suffolk, is complemented by the elegant shape of the cardinal arms. (Right) This whale at Beaulieu, Hampshire, is a traditional swell-bodied New England subject and was brought to Britain on Concorde.